# At the

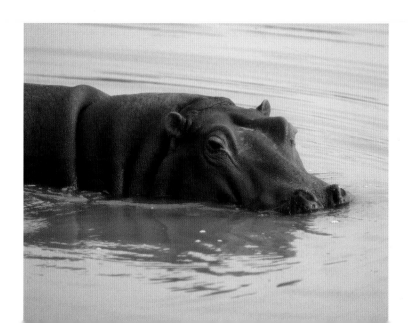

Come and see

the monkey.

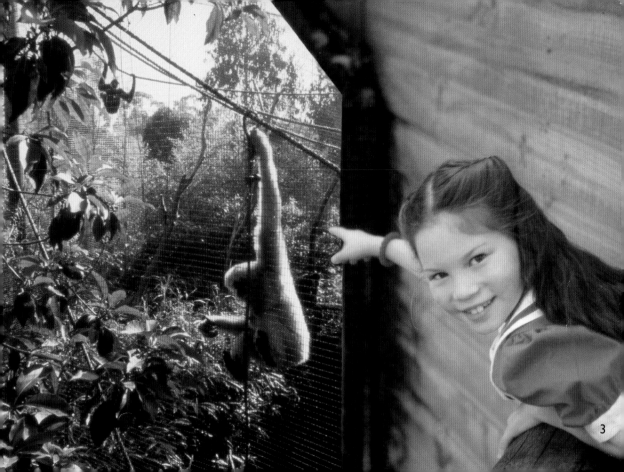

Come and see

the elephant.

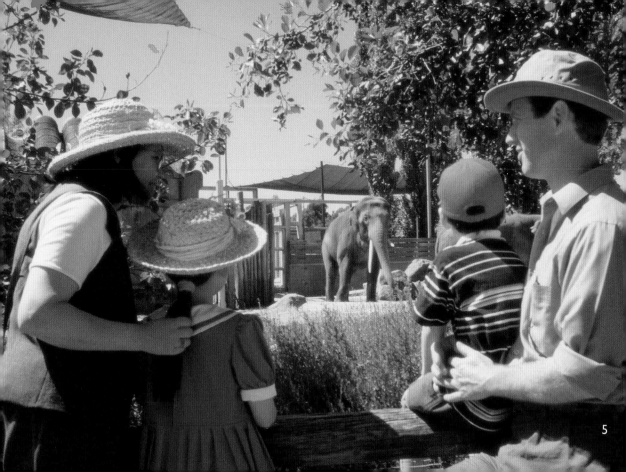

Come and see
the kangaroos.

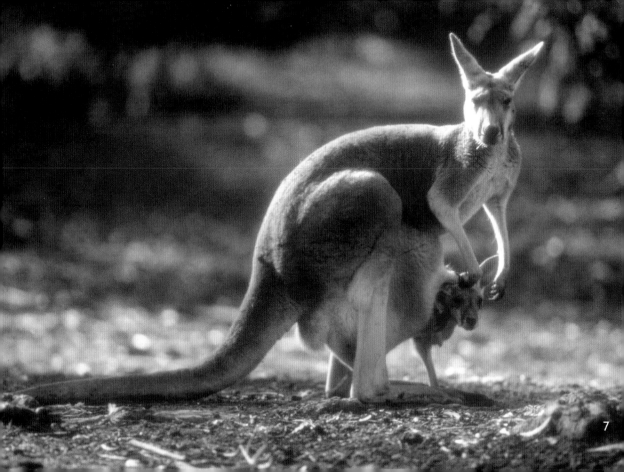

Come and see

the tiger.

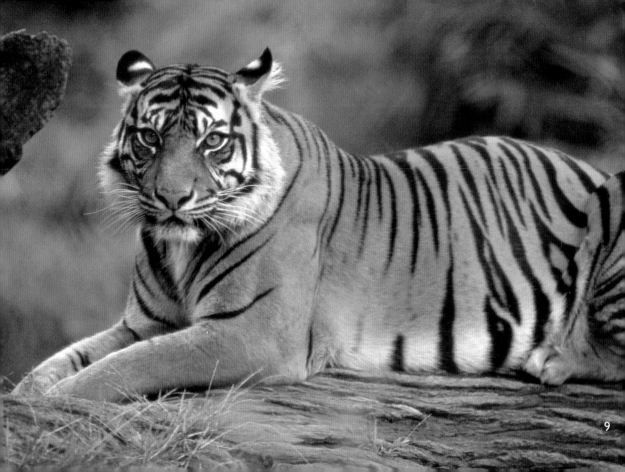

Come and see
the bear.

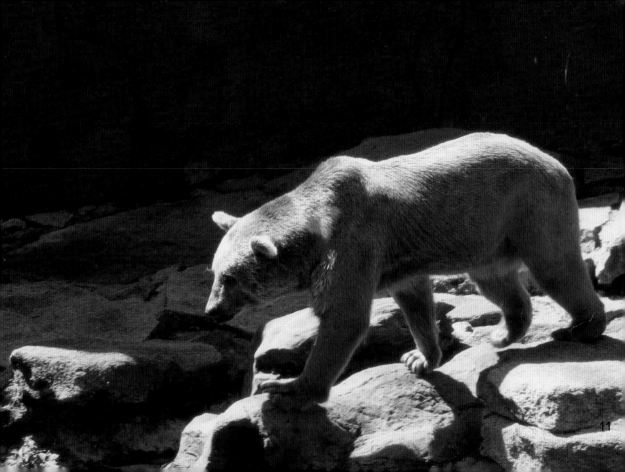

Come and see
the giraffe.

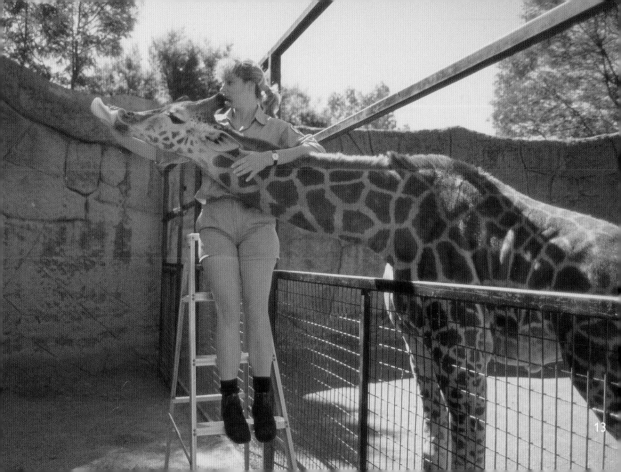

Come and see
the zebra.

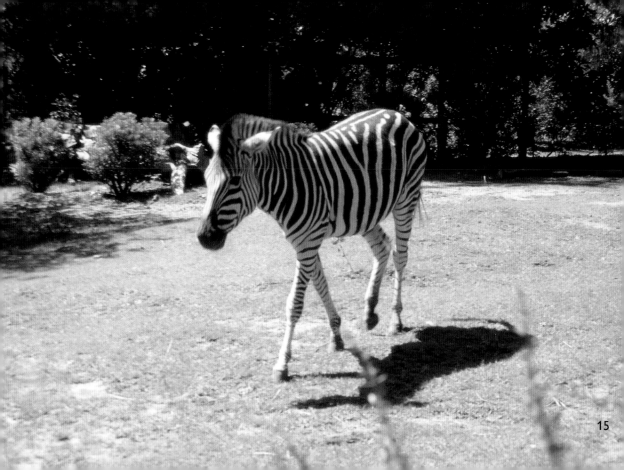

Come and see
the hippopotamus.

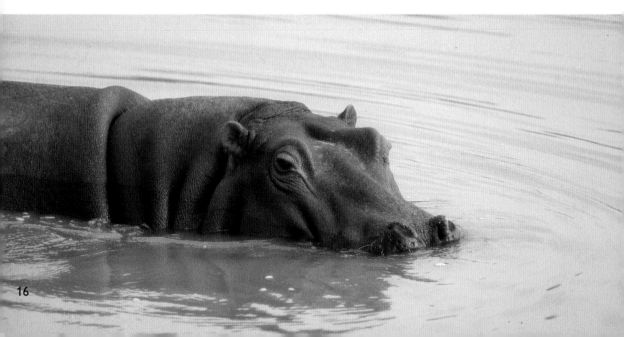